FOR MANY UNKNOWN LITTLE FRIENDS, INCLUDING MONICA

FREDERICK WARNE

Published by the Penguin Group
Registered office: 80 Strand, London, WC2R ORL
Penguin Young Readers Group, 345 Hudson Street, New York, N.Y. 10014, USA

First published 1911 by Frederick Warne
This edition with new reproductions of Beatrix Potter's book illustrations first published 2007
This edition copyright © Frederick Warne & Co. 2007
New reproductions of Beatrix Potter's book illustrations copyright © Frederick Warne & Co. 2002
Original copyright in text and illustrations © Frederick Warne & Co., 1911

Manufactured in China

THE TALE OF
TIMMY TIPTOES

BY BEATRIX POTTER

FREDERICK WARNE

ONCE upon a time there was a little fat comfortable grey squirrel, called Timmy Tiptoes. He had a nest thatched with leaves in the top of a tall tree; and he had a little squirrel wife called Goody.

Timmy Tiptoes sat out, enjoying the breeze; he whisked his tail and chuckled — "Little wife Goody, the nuts are ripe; we must lay up a store for winter and spring."

6

GOODY TIPTOES was busy pushing moss under the thatch — "The nest is so snug, we shall be sound asleep all winter." "Then we shall wake up all the thinner, when there is nothing to eat in spring-time," replied prudent Timothy.

WHEN Timmy and Goody Tiptoes came to the nut thicket, they found other squirrels were there already.

Timmy took off his jacket and hung it on a twig; they worked away quietly by themselves.

EVERY day they made several journeys and picked quantities of nuts. They carried them away in bags, and stored them in several hollow stumps near the tree where they had built their nest.

9

WHEN these stumps were full, they began
to empty the bags into a hole high up a tree,
that had belonged to a wood-pecker; the nuts
rattled down — down — down inside.

"How shall you ever get them out again? It is like
a money-box!" said Goody.

"I shall be much thinner before spring-time, my
love," said Timmy
Tiptoes, peeping
into the hole.

They did
collect quantities
— because they did
not lose them!

SQUIRRELS
who bury their
nuts in the
ground lose
more than half,
because they
cannot remember
the place.

The most
forgetful squirrel
in the wood was
called Silvertail.
He began to dig, and he could not remember.
And then he dug again and found some nuts that
did not belong to him; and there was a fight. And
other squirrels began to dig — the whole wood
was in commotion!

UNFORTUNATELY, just at this time a flock
of little birds flew by, from bush to bush,
searching for green caterpillars and spiders.
There were several sorts of little birds,
twittering different songs.

The first one sang — "Who's bin digging-up *my*
nuts? Who's-been-digging-up *my* nuts?"

And another sang —
"Little bit-a-bread
and-*no*-cheese!
Little bit-a-
bread an'-
no-cheese!"

THE
squirrels
followed
and listened.
The first
little bird
flew into the
bush where
Timmy
and Goody
Tiptoes were
quietly tying

up their bags, and
it sang — "Who's-bin digging-up *my* nuts? Who's
been digging-up *my*-nuts?"

Timmy Tiptoes went on with his work without
replying; indeed, the little bird did not expect
an answer. It was only singing its natural song,
and it meant nothing at all.

BUT when the other squirrels heard that song, they rushed upon Timmy Tiptoes and cuffed and scratched him, and upset his bag of nuts. The innocent little bird which had caused all the mischief, flew away in a fright!

Timmy rolled over and over, and then turned tail and fled towards his nest, followed by a crowd of squirrels shouting — "Who's-been digging-up *my*-nuts?"

THEY caught him and dragged him up the very same tree, where there was the little round hole, and they pushed him in. The hole was much too small for Timmy Tiptoes' figure. They squeezed him dreadfully, it was a wonder they did not break his ribs. "We will leave him here till he confesses," said Silvertail Squirrel, and he shouted into the hole —

"Who's-been-digging-up *my*-nuts?"

TIMMY TIPTOES made no reply; he had tumbled down inside the tree, upon half a peck of nuts belonging to himself. He lay quite stunned and still.

Goody Tiptoes picked up the nut bags and went home. She made a cup of tea for Timmy; but he didn't come and didn't come.

GOODY TIPTOES passed a lonely and unhappy night. Next morning she ventured back to the nut-bushes to look for him; but the other unkind squirrels drove her away.

She wandered all over the wood, calling —

"Timmy Tiptoes! Timmy Tiptoes! Oh, where is Timmy Tiptoes?"

IN the meantime Timmy Tiptoes came to his senses. He found himself tucked up in a little moss bed, very much in the dark, feeling sore; it seemed to be under ground. Timmy coughed and groaned, because his ribs hurt him. There was a chirpy noise, and a small striped Chipmunk appeared with a night light, and hoped he felt better?

It was most kind to Timmy Tiptoes; it lent him its night-cap; and the house was full of provisions.

THE
Chipmunk
explained that
it had rained
nuts through the
top of the tree —
"Besides, I found
a few buried!"
It laughed and
chuckled when
it heard Timmy's
story. While

Timmy was confined to bed, it 'ticed him to eat
quantities — "But how shall I ever get out through
that hole unless I thin myself? My wife will be
anxious!" "Just another nut — or two nuts; let me
crack them for you," said the Chipmunk. Timmy
Tiptoes grew fatter and fatter!

NOW Goody Tiptoes had set to work again
by herself. She did not put any more nuts into
the wood-pecker's hole, because she had always
doubted how
they could
be got out
again. She hid
them under
a tree root;
they rattled
down, down,
down. Once
when Goody
emptied an
extra big
bagful, there

was a decided squeak; and next time Goody
brought another bagful, a little striped
Chipmunk scrambled out in a hurry.

"IT is getting perfectly full-up downstairs; the sitting-room is full, and they are rolling along the passage; and my husband, Chippy Hackee, has run away and left me. What is the explanation of these showers of nuts?"

"I am sure I beg your pardon; I did not know that anybody lived here," said Mrs. Goody Tiptoes; "but where is Chippy Hackee? My husband, Timmy Tiptoes, has run away too."

"I know where Chippy is; a little bird told me," said Mrs. Chippy Hackee.

SHE led the way to the wood-pecker's tree, and they listened at the hole.

Down below there was a noise of nut crackers, and a fat squirrel voice and a thin squirrel voice were singing together —

"My little old man and I fell out,
　How shall we bring this matter about?
　Bring it about as well as you can,
　And get you gone, you little old man!"

"YOU could squeeze in, through that little round hole," said Goody Tiptoes. "Yes, I could," said the Chipmunk, "but my husband, Chippy Hackee, bites!"

Down below there was a noise of cracking nuts and nibbling; and then the fat squirrel voice and the thin squirrel voice sang —

"For the diddlum day
  Day diddle dum di!
  Day diddle diddle dum day!"

THEN Goody peeped in at the hole, and called down — "Timmy Tiptoes! Oh fie, Timmy Tiptoes!" And Timmy replied, "Is that you, Goody Tiptoes? Why, certainly!"

He came up and kissed Goody through the hole; but he was so fat that he could not get out.

Chippy Hackee was not too fat, but he did not want to come; he stayed down below and chuckled.

AND so it went on for a fortnight; till a big wind blew off the top of the tree, and opened up the hole and let in the rain.

Then Timmy Tiptoes came out, and went home with an umbrella.

BUT Chippy Hackee continued to camp out for another week, although it was uncomfortable.

AT last a large bear came walking through the wood. Perhaps he also was looking for nuts; he seemed to be sniffing around.

Chippy Hackee went home in a hurry!

AND when Chippy Hackee got home, he found he had caught a cold in his head; and he was more uncomfortable still.

And now Timmy and Goody Tiptoes keep their nut-store fastened up with a little padlock.

AND whenever that little bird sees the
Chipmunks, he sings — "Who's-been-digging-up
my-nuts? Who's been digging-up *my*-nuts?" But
nobody ever answers!